Gluten-Free Chocolate Cookie Recipes

Indulge in Decadent Chocolate Flavors Without Gluten

While every precaution has been taken in the preparation of this book, the publisher assumes no responsibility for errors or omissions, or for damages resulting from the use of the information contained herein.

GLUTEN-FREE CHOCOLATE COOKIE RECIPES

First edition. December 2, 2023.

Copyright © 2023 john ahmad.

ISBN: 979-8223448761

Written by john ahmad.

John Ahmad

Chapter Outline:

Understanding Gluten-Free Baking

- What is Gluten and Why Go Gluten-Free?
- Basics of Gluten-Free Baking
- Gluten-Free Flour Substitutes
- Xanthan Gum and Binding Agents

Essential Ingredients for Gluten-Free Chocolate Cookies

- Exploring Gluten-Free Flours
- Natural Sweeteners for Healthier Cookies
- Dairy-Free Alternatives
- Boosting Flavor with Extracts and Spices

Baking Techniques and Tips

- Measuring Gluten-Free Flours Correctly
- Achieving the Right Cookie Texture
- Mixing and Incorporating Ingredients
- Troubleshooting Common Gluten-Free Baking Issues

Classic Chocolate Chip Cookies

- Traditional Chocolate Chip Cookie Recipe
- Variations: Dark Chocolate Chips, Mini Morsels, etc.
- Adding Nuts for Crunch and Flavor
- Creating Giant Chocolate Chip Cookies

Double Chocolate Delights

- Rich Cocoa-Based Cookie Dough
- Incorporating Different Types of Chocolate
- Chocolate-Stuffed Cookies
- Melting Chocolate for Dipping and Drizzling

Fudgy Brownie Cookies

- Combining the Best of Cookies and Brownies
- Achieving a Chewy and Fudgy Texture
- Incorporating Add-Ins: Walnuts, Marshmallows, etc.
- Brownie Cookie Sundaes and Ice Cream Sandwiches

White Chocolate Macadamia Nut Treats

- Creamy White Chocolate and Nutty Macadamias
- Balancing Sweetness with Tart Ingredients
- Macadamia Nut Flour for Unique Flavor
- White Chocolate Dipping Techniques

Mint Chocolate Chip Cookies

- Infusing Mint Flavor into Cookies
- Achieving a Refreshing and Chocolatey Balance
- Natural Coloring with Fresh Mint Leaves
- Mint Chocolate Sandwich Cookies

Chocolate Peanut Butter Swirl Cookies

- Marbling Techniques for Stunning Cookies
- Making Homemade Peanut Butter Swirls
- Achieving the Perfect Sweet-Savory Harmony
- No-Bake Chocolate Peanut Butter Cookies

Sea Salt and Dark Chocolate Shortbread

- Elevating Flavors with Sea Salt
- Creating Buttery and Crumbly Shortbread
- Choosing the Right Dark Chocolate Percentage
- Shortbread Dipping and Drizzling

Chocolate Oatmeal No-Bake Cookies

- Easy No-Bake Cookie Recipe
- Incorporating Rolled Oats for Texture
- No-Bake Variations with Coconut, Nuts, and Fruits
- Quick and Decadent Chocolate Fix

Decadent Chocolate Avocado Cookies

- Using Avocado for Creaminess and Healthiness
- Hiding Nutrients in Delicious Cookies
- Balancing Chocolate and Avocado Flavors
- Avocado Frosting and Fillings

Gluten-Free Chocolate Sandwich Cookies

- Creating Cookie Sandwiches with Gluten-Free Biscuits
- Different Types of Fillings: Cream, Ganache, etc.
- Assembling and Decorating Cookie Sandwiches
- Mini Cookie Sandwiches for Parties

Chocolate Espresso Bites

- Adding Coffee Flavor for Depth
- Incorporating Espresso Powder into Dough
- Creating Chocolate Coffee Glazes
- Espresso-Chocolate Energy Bites

Hazelnut Chocolate Thumbprint Cookies

- Crafting Thumbprint Indents for Fillings
- Nutella and Hazelnut Fillings
- Toasting Hazelnuts for Enhanced Flavor
- Hazelnut Chocolate Thumbprint Cookie Variations

Vegan Chocolate Coconut Cookies

- Dairy-Free Chocolate and Coconut Creations
- Coconut Milk and Oil in Vegan Baking
- Vegan Chocolate Ganache and Icing
- Coconut Whipped Cream for Toppings

Chocolate Protein Power Cookies

- Incorporating Protein-Rich Ingredients
- Balancing Taste and Nutrition
- Protein Powder in Gluten-Free Baking
- Post-Workout Chocolate Protein Cookies

Flourless Chocolate Almond Cookies

- Almond Flour as a Gluten-Free Base
- Nut Butters for Flavor and Texture
- Almond Extract and Enhancing Almond Flavor
- Flourless Almond Joy-Inspired Cookies

Mexican Hot Chocolate Snickerdoodles

- Spices for a Warm and Spicy Twist
- Creating the Perfect Snickerdoodle Coating
- Chocolate and Cinnamon Flavor Harmony
- Spicy Chocolate Cookie Pairings

Celebratory Chocolate Sprinkle Cookies

- Festive and Colorful Sprinkle Decorations
- Incorporating Sprinkles into the Dough
- Personalized Sprinkle Blends
- Sprinkle-Filled Pinata Cookies for Parties

Chapter 1: Understanding Gluten-Free Baking

Baking delicious and satisfying gluten-free chocolate cookies requires a basic understanding of gluten and the principles behind gluten-free baking. Whether you're new to gluten-free baking or simply looking to perfect your techniques, this chapter will provide you with essential knowledge and insights to set you up for success.

What is Gluten and Why Go Gluten-Free?

Gluten is a protein composite found in wheat, barley, and rye. It's responsible for the elasticity and structure of many baked goods, giving them that chewy texture we love. However, for those with celiac disease, non-celiac gluten sensitivity, or those opting for a gluten-free lifestyle, consuming gluten can lead to various health issues.

By going gluten-free, you can still enjoy delectable treats without sacrificing taste and texture. With the right ingredients and techniques, you can create mouthwatering chocolate cookies that are safe for everyone to enjoy.

Basics of Gluten-Free Baking

When adapting traditional cookie recipes to gluten-free versions, it's important to understand the unique properties of gluten-free flours. These flours lack the binding and elasticity of wheat flour, which can affect the final texture of your cookies. Common gluten-free flours include almond flour, coconut flour, rice flour, oat flour, and tapioca flour.

Gluten-Free Flour Substitutes

Experiment with different gluten-free flours to find the perfect combination that suits your preferences. For instance, almond flour imparts a rich nuttiness, while coconut flour provides moisture. Combining flours can help mimic the texture of all-purpose wheat flour.

To enhance the binding properties of gluten-free dough, consider using xanthan gum or guar gum.

Xanthan Gum and Binding Agents

Xanthan gum is a popular gluten-free baking additive that acts as a binder and thickener. It helps improve the texture of baked goods by mimicking the elasticity of gluten. When using xanthan gum, start with a small amount (usually 1/4 teaspoon per cup of gluten-free flour) to avoid over-gumminess. Guar gum is another alternative that achieves similar results.

Arming yourself with the basics of gluten-free baking is the first step toward creating irresistible chocolate cookies that are safe for all to enjoy. By understanding the role of gluten in traditional baking and discovering the potential of gluten-free flours and binders, you're well on your way to mastering the art of gluten-free chocolate cookie baking.

In the next chapter, we'll delve into the essential ingredients you'll need for crafting mouthwatering gluten-free chocolate cookies that are both flavorful and satisfying.

Chapter 2: Essential Ingredients for Gluten-Free Chocolate Cookies

Creating truly delectable gluten-free chocolate cookies is an art that revolves around the careful selection of ingredients. This chapter is your guide to assembling the perfect lineup of elements that will bring exceptional flavor, texture, and overall satisfaction to your cookies.

Exploring Gluten-Free Flours

Almond Flour: Almond flour, made from finely ground almonds, is a beloved staple in gluten-free baking. Its slightly nutty and rich flavor adds depth to chocolate cookies. Its moisture content can, however, make cookies softer, so it's often used in combination with other flours.

Coconut Flour: Known for its unique absorbent qualities, coconut flour has a natural sweetness and imparts a delightful, subtle coconut flavor. It's highly absorbent, so be sure to use it in moderation and increase liquid ingredients to maintain the right consistency.

Rice Flour: Derived from rice grains, this mild-flavored flour is a versatile choice. It's excellent for achieving a balanced texture and works well in combination with other flours to avoid graininess.

Oat Flour: Ground from whole oats, oat flour introduces a hearty, slightly earthy taste to your cookies. It provides a denser texture and is fantastic for recipes that benefit from a robust, nutty flavor.

Tapioca Flour: Extracted from the cassava root, tapioca flour contributes chewiness and binding properties to your cookies. It's often used in small amounts to improve the texture of gluten-free baked goods.

Natural Sweeteners for Healthier Cookies

Maple Syrup: Maple syrup brings a natural sweetness and a subtle hint of caramel to your cookies. Its liquid consistency adds moisture to the dough and complements the chocolate flavors wonderfully.

Honey: As a natural sweetener, honey lends a unique floral note to your cookies. Its viscosity and hygroscopic nature help keep cookies moist and tender.

Coconut Sugar: With its lower glycemic index and rich taste reminiscent of brown sugar, coconut sugar adds a warm, caramel-like flavor to your cookies.

Date Syrup: Made from pureed dates, this syrup infuses your cookies with a rich sweetness and a touch of earthiness, providing a unique twist to traditional flavors.

Dairy-Free Alternatives

Coconut Oil: Often used as a butter substitute, coconut oil adds a pleasant coconut aroma and flavor to your cookies. Its solid state at room temperature ensures a desirable cookie texture.

Nut Butters: Almond, peanut, and cashew butters introduce creamy richness and a nutty undertone to your cookies. They also contribute healthy fats that enhance both flavor and texture.

Non-Dairy Milk: Almond, soy, oat, and coconut milk are excellent dairy milk alternatives. They bring their own subtle flavors to the mix and work well in moistening the dough.

Vegan Butter: Plant-based margarines and spreads mimic the taste and texture of butter in your cookies. Choose varieties with high fat content for the best results.

Boosting Flavor with Extracts and Spices

Vanilla Extract: A pantry staple, vanilla extract adds warmth and complexity to your cookie's flavor profile. Choose pure vanilla extract for the best results.

Almond Extract: Almond extract is a secret weapon for enhancing nutty flavors in your cookies. Use it sparingly to avoid overpowering the other ingredients.

Cinnamon: Ground cinnamon infuses your cookies with a comforting warmth. It pairs exceptionally well with the rich chocolate taste.

Sea Salt: A pinch of sea salt can elevate the sweetness of your cookies and intensify the chocolate experience. It's a secret ingredient that makes flavors pop.

Crafting the perfect batch of gluten-free chocolate cookies requires a thoughtful selection of ingredients. Each element plays a vital role in determining the final taste, texture, and overall satisfaction of your creations. As you explore different combinations and experiment with varying proportions, you'll unlock the secrets to making gluten-free cookies that are truly extraordinary.

In the next chapter, we'll dive into the essential baking techniques and tips that will empower you to create impeccable gluten-free chocolate cookies every single time.

Chapter 3: Baking Techniques and Tips

Achieving the perfect batch of gluten-free chocolate cookies is a blend of art and science. In this chapter, we'll delve into essential techniques and tips that will empower you to create cookies with impeccable taste, texture, and appearance. From accurate measurements to troubleshooting common issues, you'll be well-equipped to tackle any baking challenge.

Measuring Gluten-Free Flours Correctly

Accurate measurements are crucial in gluten-free baking, as different flours have varying weights and moisture content. Use dry measuring cups for flours and spoon them gently into the cup, then level off with a flat edge. Avoid tapping or shaking the cup to prevent compacting the flour.

Achieving the Right Cookie Texture

Chill the Dough: Refrigerating the dough for at least 30 minutes before baking helps solidify the fats, resulting in cookies with a better shape and texture.

Scoop Uniformly: Use a cookie scoop for consistent cookie size. This ensures even baking and a uniform appearance.

Watch the Oven: Gluten-free cookies can go from perfectly baked to overdone quickly. Keep a close eye on your cookies during the last few minutes of baking.

Mixing and Incorporating Ingredients

Room Temperature Ingredients: Use room temperature eggs and dairy alternatives to ensure proper emulsification and even distribution of fats.

Mix Gradually: When incorporating dry ingredients into wet, add them gradually and mix until just combined. Overmixing can result in tough cookies.

Fold in Mix-Ins: Whether it's chocolate chips, nuts, or dried fruits, fold in mix-ins gently to prevent them from sinking to the bottom.

Troubleshooting Common Gluten-Free Baking Issues

Cookies Spread Too Much: If your cookies are spreading excessively, the dough might be too warm. Try chilling it before baking.

Cookies are Dry or Crumbly: Overbaking or using too much flour can result in dry cookies. Check for proper measurements and avoid overmixing.

Cookies are Gritty: Coarse textures can result from using a flour with a coarse grind. Opt for finer flours or use a blend to achieve a smoother texture.

Cookies Are Too Soft: If your cookies are too soft after cooling, they might need a bit more time in the oven or a longer cooling period on the baking sheet.

Mastering the techniques and tips outlined in this chapter will elevate your gluten-free chocolate cookie game. From properly measuring flours to troubleshooting common baking dilemmas, you're equipped to create cookies that boast optimal taste, texture, and appearance.

In the next chapter, we're diving into the classics with "Classic Chocolate Chip Cookies." Get ready to create a gluten-free version of this timeless favorite that rivals its traditional counterpart.

Chapter 4: Classic Chocolate Chip Cookies

In the world of cookies, few recipes hold as much nostalgia and universal appeal as the classic chocolate chip cookie. In this chapter, we'll explore how to create these timeless treats in a gluten-free version that retains all the charm and deliciousness of the original.

Traditional Chocolate Chip Cookie Recipe

Ingredients:

- 1 cup gluten-free all-purpose flour
- 1/2 teaspoon baking soda
- 1/4 teaspoon salt
- 1/2 cup unsalted butter, softened
- 1/2 cup granulated sugar
- 1/2 cup packed brown sugar
- 1 large egg
- 1 teaspoon pure vanilla extract
- 1 cup gluten-free chocolate chips

Instructions:

1. Preheat your oven to 350°F (175°C) and line a baking sheet with parchment paper.
2. In a medium bowl, whisk together the gluten-free flour, baking soda, and salt.
3. In a separate larger bowl, cream together the softened butter, granulated sugar, and brown sugar until light and fluffy.
4. Beat in the egg and vanilla extract until well combined.
5. Gradually add the dry ingredients to the wet ingredients, mixing until just combined.
6. Fold in the gluten-free chocolate chips.

7. Drop spoonfuls of dough onto the prepared baking sheet, spacing them about 2 inches apart.
8. Bake for 10-12 minutes or until the edges are golden brown. The centers may look slightly underdone, but they will firm up as they cool.
9. Allow the cookies to cool on the baking sheet for a few minutes before transferring them to a wire rack to cool completely.

Variations: Dark Chocolate Chips, Mini Morsels, etc.

Dark Chocolate Chips: For an intense chocolate experience, replace the standard chocolate chips with dark chocolate chips. The deeper cocoa flavor will complement the cookie's sweetness.

Mini Chocolate Chips: Using mini chocolate chips can create a more even distribution of chocolate throughout the cookie, resulting in every bite being full of chocolatey goodness.

Adding Nuts for Crunch and Flavor

Chopped Walnuts: Walnuts add a satisfying crunch and a nutty flavor that pairs exceptionally well with the chocolate. Fold them into the dough for a delightful contrast.

Pecans: Pecans bring a slightly buttery and rich flavor to your cookies. Toast them before adding to intensify their nuttiness.

Creating Giant Chocolate Chip Cookies

For a truly indulgent treat, consider making giant chocolate chip cookies. Follow the same recipe, but use a larger cookie scoop to create bigger portions of dough. Bake them a bit longer, typically around 15-18 minutes, until the edges are deeply golden and the centers are set.

Mastering the art of classic chocolate chip cookies in a gluten-free form is a true accomplishment. The perfect blend of chewy and crisp textures, combined with the sweet and chocolatey goodness, will leave you and your guests craving for more. In the next chapter, we'll dive into an intense chocolate experience with "Double Chocolate Delights."

Chapter 5: Double Chocolate Delights

When one type of chocolate just isn't enough, it's time to dive into the world of double chocolate delights. In this chapter, we'll explore the art of crafting gluten-free cookies that are rich in cocoa and bursting with a symphony of chocolate flavors.

Rich Cocoa-Based Cookie Dough

Ingredients:

- 1 cup gluten-free all-purpose flour
- 1/3 cup unsweetened cocoa powder
- 1/2 teaspoon baking soda
- 1/4 teaspoon salt
- 1/2 cup unsalted butter, softened
- 3/4 cup granulated sugar
- 1 large egg
- 1 teaspoon pure vanilla extract
- 1/2 cup gluten-free chocolate chips

Instructions:

1. Preheat your oven to 350°F (175°C) and line a baking sheet with parchment paper.
2. In a medium bowl, whisk together the gluten-free flour, cocoa powder, baking soda, and salt.
3. In a separate larger bowl, cream together the softened butter and granulated sugar until light and fluffy.
4. Beat in the egg and vanilla extract until well combined.
5. Gradually add the dry ingredients to the wet ingredients, mixing until just combined.
6. Fold in the gluten-free chocolate chips.
7. Drop spoonfuls of dough onto the prepared baking sheet,

spacing them about 2 inches apart.

8. Bake for 10-12 minutes or until the edges are set. The centers may look slightly underdone, but they will firm up as they cool.
9. Allow the cookies to cool on the baking sheet for a few minutes before transferring them to a wire rack to cool completely.

Incorporating Different Types of Chocolate

White Chocolate Chips: For a striking contrast, mix in white chocolate chips with the dark cocoa-based dough. The creamy sweetness of white chocolate complements the rich cocoa flavor.

Milk Chocolate Chunks: Incorporating milk chocolate chunks adds a velvety and nostalgic twist to your cookies. The sweeter and creamier profile of milk chocolate pairs beautifully with the cocoa dough.

Chocolate-Stuffed Cookies

Take your double chocolate cookies to the next level by creating chocolate-stuffed versions:

Chocolate Truffle Filling: Roll small amounts of chocolate ganache into balls and encase them in cookie dough. As the cookies bake, the ganache will melt into a luscious surprise.

Molten Lava Cookies: Create a pocket of chocolate in the center of each cookie dough ball. As the cookies bake, the chocolate will melt, creating a gooey and indulgent center.

Melting Chocolate for Dipping and Drizzling

Use high-quality gluten-free chocolate for dipping and drizzling:

1. Chop the chocolate into small pieces for even melting.
2. Microwave in 20-second intervals, stirring between each interval, until smooth and melted.
3. Dip cooled cookies into the melted chocolate, allowing excess to drip off, and place on parchment paper to set.
4. Drizzle the melted chocolate over cookies using a fork or a piping bag for a decorative touch.

Double chocolate delights are a testament to the irresistible allure of cocoa in all its forms. By creating cookies that boast a cocoa-rich dough, a harmonious blend of chocolate types, and even surprise pockets of molten chocolate, you're elevating the cookie experience to a new level of indulgence. In the next chapter, we'll explore the marriage of two beloved flavors in "Mint Chocolate Chip Cookies."

Chapter 6: Fudgy Brownie Cookies

Prepare to embark on a journey that merges the irresistible qualities of brownies and cookies. In this chapter, we'll explore the art of crafting gluten-free cookies that boast the chewy, fudgy texture of brownies, creating a delightful treat that's the best of both worlds.

Combining the Best of Cookies and Brownies

Ingredients:

- 1/2 cup gluten-free all-purpose flour
- 1/4 cup unsweetened cocoa powder
- 1/4 teaspoon baking powder
- 1/4 teaspoon salt
- 1/2 cup semisweet or dark chocolate chips
- 2 tablespoons unsalted butter
- 1/4 cup granulated sugar
- 1/4 cup packed brown sugar
- 2 large eggs
- 1 teaspoon pure vanilla extract

Instructions:

1. Preheat your oven to 350°F (175°C) and line a baking sheet with parchment paper.
2. In a small bowl, whisk together the gluten-free flour, cocoa powder, baking powder, and salt.
3. In a heatproof bowl, melt the chocolate chips and butter together. You can use a microwave in 20-second intervals or a double boiler on the stovetop. Stir until smooth.
4. In a separate bowl, whisk together the granulated sugar, brown sugar, eggs, and vanilla extract until well combined.
5. Gradually add the melted chocolate mixture to the sugar and

egg mixture, stirring until smooth.

6. Gently fold in the dry ingredients until just combined.

7. Drop spoonfuls of dough onto the prepared baking sheet, spacing them about 2 inches apart.

8. Bake for 10-12 minutes or until the edges are set and the tops are slightly cracked. The centers should still be slightly soft.

9. Allow the cookies to cool on the baking sheet for a few minutes before transferring them to a wire rack to cool completely.

Achieving a Chewy and Fudgy Texture

Underbaking: To achieve that beloved brownie-like texture, slightly underbake the cookies. The centers should be soft and fudgy, resembling the interior of a brownie.

Moisture Content: The moisture content of these cookies is key to their fudginess. Be sure not to overbake them to maintain the desired chewiness.

Incorporating Add-Ins: Walnuts, Marshmallows, etc.

Chopped Walnuts: For a textural contrast, fold in chopped walnuts into the dough. They add a satisfying crunch that complements the fudgy center.

Mini Marshmallows: Incorporate mini marshmallows to recreate the experience of a s'mores-inspired brownie. They'll melt slightly during baking, creating gooey pockets of sweetness.

Brownie Cookie Sundaes and Ice Cream Sandwiches

Transform your fudgy brownie cookies into delectable desserts:

Brownie Cookie Sundaes: Layer scoops of vanilla ice cream between two brownie cookies, and drizzle with chocolate sauce and whipped cream for a decadent sundae.

Ice Cream Sandwiches: Pair two brownie cookies with a scoop of your favorite ice cream for a delightful ice cream sandwich.

Fudgy brownie cookies are a dream come true for anyone who adores the chewy texture and intense flavor of brownies. By merging the attributes of cookies and brownies, you're creating a treat that satisfies both cravings. In the next chapter, we'll explore the elegant pairing of flavors in "White Chocolate Macadamia Nut Treats."

Chapter 7: White Chocolate Macadamia Nut Treats

Indulgence takes a new form with the elegant pairing of creamy white chocolate and buttery macadamia nuts. In this chapter, we'll delve into the creation of gluten-free cookies that capture the delicate balance between sweetness and the rich, nutty flavors of macadamias.

Creamy White Chocolate and Nutty Macadamias

Ingredients:

- 1 cup gluten-free all-purpose flour
- 1/2 teaspoon baking soda
- 1/4 teaspoon salt
- 1/2 cup unsalted butter, softened
- 1/2 cup granulated sugar
- 1/4 cup packed brown sugar
- 1 large egg
- 1 teaspoon pure vanilla extract
- 1/2 cup white chocolate chips
- 1/2 cup chopped macadamia nuts

Instructions:

1. Preheat your oven to 350°F (175°C) and line a baking sheet with parchment paper.
2. In a medium bowl, whisk together the gluten-free flour, baking soda, and salt.
3. In a separate larger bowl, cream together the softened butter, granulated sugar, and brown sugar until light and fluffy.
4. Beat in the egg and vanilla extract until well combined.
5. Gradually add the dry ingredients to the wet ingredients, mixing until just combined.

6. Fold in the white chocolate chips and chopped macadamia nuts.
7. Drop spoonfuls of dough onto the prepared baking sheet, spacing them about 2 inches apart.
8. Bake for 10-12 minutes or until the edges are golden brown. The centers may look slightly underdone, but they will firm up as they cool.
9. Allow the cookies to cool on the baking sheet for a few minutes before transferring them to a wire rack to cool completely.

Balancing Sweetness with Tart Ingredients

Dried Cranberries: Add a touch of tartness by folding in dried cranberries. Their burst of bright flavor creates a harmonious contrast with the sweet white chocolate.

Lemon Zest: Incorporating lemon zest into the cookie dough infuses a citrusy aroma and tangy undertone that complements the sweetness.

Macadamia Nut Flour for Unique Flavor

Substitute a portion of the all-purpose flour with macadamia nut flour for a unique twist:

1. Grind macadamia nuts until finely powdered.
2. Replace about 1/4 cup of the all-purpose flour with an equal amount of macadamia nut flour.
3. Proceed with the rest of the recipe as usual.

White Chocolate Dipping Techniques

Use high-quality white chocolate for dipping:

1. Chop the white chocolate into small pieces for even melting.
2. Microwave in 20-second intervals, stirring between each interval, until smooth and melted.
3. Dip cooled cookies into the melted white chocolate, allowing excess to drip off, and place on parchment paper to set.
4. Drizzle the melted white chocolate over cookies for an elegant touch.

White chocolate macadamia nut treats embody a luxurious symphony of flavors and textures. With the creamy sweetness of white chocolate and the buttery richness of macadamia nuts, you're creating cookies that are both sophisticated and utterly delightful. In the next chapter, we'll explore a refreshing twist with "Mint Chocolate Chip Cookies."

Chapter 8: Mint Chocolate Chip Cookies

Prepare to embark on a refreshing journey that combines the invigorating essence of mint with the indulgent allure of chocolate. In this chapter, we'll explore the art of crafting gluten-free cookies that exude a delightful balance between minty freshness and rich chocolatey goodness.

Infusing Mint Flavor into Cookies
Ingredients:

- 1 cup gluten-free all-purpose flour
- 1/2 teaspoon baking soda
- 1/4 teaspoon salt
- 1/2 cup unsalted butter, softened
- 1/2 cup granulated sugar
- 1/4 cup packed brown sugar
- 1 large egg
- 1 teaspoon pure peppermint extract
- Green food coloring (optional)
- 1/2 cup gluten-free chocolate chips

Instructions:

1. Preheat your oven to 350°F (175°C) and line a baking sheet with parchment paper.
2. In a medium bowl, whisk together the gluten-free flour, baking soda, and salt.
3. In a separate larger bowl, cream together the softened butter, granulated sugar, and brown sugar until light and fluffy.
4. Beat in the egg and peppermint extract until well combined.
5. If desired, add a few drops of green food coloring to achieve a minty hue in your cookies. Mix well.

6. Gradually add the dry ingredients to the wet ingredients, mixing until just combined.
7. Fold in the gluten-free chocolate chips.
8. Drop spoonfuls of dough onto the prepared baking sheet, spacing them about 2 inches apart.
9. Bake for 10-12 minutes or until the edges are golden brown. The centers may look slightly underdone, but they will firm up as they cool.
10. Allow the cookies to cool on the baking sheet for a few minutes before transferring them to a wire rack to cool completely.

Achieving a Refreshing and Chocolatey Balance

Peppermint Extract: The key to achieving the right level of minty freshness is using pure peppermint extract. It delivers a clean and invigorating flavor.

Chocolate Balance: The chocolate chips provide a decadent contrast to the minty notes. Be sure to choose high-quality gluten-free chocolate chips for the best flavor.

Natural Coloring with Fresh Mint Leaves

Fresh Mint Leaves: For a natural approach to coloring, finely chop fresh mint leaves and add them to the cookie dough. The green flecks will lend a beautiful hue while infusing a subtle mint flavor.

Mint Chocolate Sandwich Cookies

Take your mint chocolate cookies to the next level by creating mint chocolate sandwich cookies:

Mint Cream Filling: Whip together butter, powdered sugar, and a touch of peppermint extract to create a creamy filling. Sandwich it between two mint chocolate chip cookies for an irresistible treat.

Chapter 9: Chocolate Peanut Butter Swirl Cookies

Prepare to experience the delightful combination of rich chocolate and creamy peanut butter in a mesmerizing swirl. In this chapter, we'll explore the art of crafting gluten-free cookies that feature the enchanting harmony of these two beloved flavors.

Marbling Techniques for Stunning Cookies

Ingredients:

- 1 cup gluten-free all-purpose flour
- 1/2 teaspoon baking soda
- 1/4 teaspoon salt
- 1/2 cup unsalted butter, softened
- 1/2 cup granulated sugar
- 1/4 cup packed brown sugar
- 1 large egg
- 1 teaspoon pure vanilla extract
- 1/4 cup unsweetened cocoa powder
- 1/4 cup creamy peanut butter

Instructions:

1. Preheat your oven to 350°F (175°C) and line a baking sheet with parchment paper.
2. In a medium bowl, whisk together the gluten-free flour, baking soda, and salt.
3. In a separate larger bowl, cream together the softened butter, granulated sugar, and brown sugar until light and fluffy.
4. Beat in the egg and vanilla extract until well combined.
5. Gradually add the dry ingredients to the wet ingredients, mixing until just combined.

6. Divide the dough in half. Leave one half plain, and mix the other half with unsweetened cocoa powder to create chocolate dough.
7. Take a tablespoon of plain dough and a tablespoon of chocolate dough. Roll them into separate balls.
8. Flatten each ball slightly and then press them together, creating a marbled effect. Roll the combined dough into a ball.
9. Drop spoonfuls of marbled dough onto the prepared baking sheet, spacing them about 2 inches apart.
10. Bake for 10-12 minutes or until the edges are golden brown. The centers may look slightly underdone, but they will firm up as they cool.
11. Allow the cookies to cool on the baking sheet for a few minutes before transferring them to a wire rack to cool completely.

Making Homemade Peanut Butter Swirls

Create Peanut Butter Ribbon: Warm up creamy peanut butter slightly to make it more malleable. Use a spoon to create a swirl of peanut butter on top of the cookie dough before baking. Gently press the peanut butter into the dough to ensure it adheres.

Achieving the Perfect Sweet-Savory Harmony

Peanut Butter Flavor: The natural nuttiness of peanut butter complements the sweetness of the cookie dough. Be sure to use creamy peanut butter for a smooth and consistent swirl.

Balanced Marbling: Achieve a balanced marbling effect by using equal parts plain dough and chocolate dough. This ensures that both flavors shine through.

No-Bake Chocolate Peanut Butter Cookies
Create a no-bake version of these flavors:
Ingredients:

- 1/2 cup creamy peanut butter
- 1/4 cup honey or maple syrup
- 1/4 cup unsweetened cocoa powder
- 1/4 cup gluten-free oats
- 1/4 cup chopped peanuts

Instructions:

1. In a mixing bowl, combine peanut butter and honey or maple syrup.
2. Stir in cocoa powder until well mixed.
3. Add gluten-free oats and chopped peanuts, mixing until combined.
4. Drop spoonfuls of the mixture onto parchment paper and flatten slightly to create cookies.
5. Place in the refrigerator or freezer to set.

Chapter 10: Sea Salt and Dark Chocolate Shortbread

Prepare to indulge in the exquisite harmony of rich dark chocolate and the delicate touch of sea salt, all encapsulated in a buttery and crumbly shortbread cookie. In this chapter, we'll explore the art of crafting gluten-free shortbread cookies that deliver a symphony of flavors.

Elevating Flavors with Sea Salt

Ingredients:

- 1 1/2 cups gluten-free all-purpose flour
- 1/4 teaspoon salt
- 1/2 cup unsalted butter, softened
- 1/3 cup powdered sugar
- 1 teaspoon pure vanilla extract
- 3 oz dark chocolate (70-80% cocoa), chopped
- Coarse sea salt, for sprinkling

Instructions:

1. Preheat your oven to 325°F (160°C) and line a baking sheet with parchment paper.
2. In a medium bowl, whisk together the gluten-free flour and salt.
3. In a separate larger bowl, cream together the softened butter and powdered sugar until smooth and creamy.
4. Beat in the vanilla extract until well combined.
5. Gradually add the dry ingredients to the wet ingredients, mixing until a dough forms.
6. Gently fold in the chopped dark chocolate until evenly distributed.
7. Roll out the dough on a lightly floured surface to about 1/4-inch thickness.

8. Use cookie cutters to cut out desired shapes and place them on the prepared baking sheet.

9. Sprinkle a pinch of coarse sea salt over each cookie.

10. Bake for 12-15 minutes or until the edges are golden. The centers should remain pale.

11. Allow the cookies to cool on the baking sheet for a few minutes before transferring them to a wire rack to cool completely.

Creating Buttery and Crumbly Shortbread

Cold Butter: Use cold butter that's been cut into small pieces. This ensures a flaky and crumbly texture.

Gentle Mixing: Avoid overmixing the dough. Mix until the ingredients come together, and the dough can be formed.

Choosing the Right Dark Chocolate Percentage

Dark Chocolate Variety: Choose dark chocolate with a cocoa percentage between 70-80%. This range provides a perfect balance of chocolate intensity and sweetness.

Chopping Chocolate: Chop the dark chocolate into small pieces for even distribution throughout the shortbread.

Shortbread Dipping and Drizzling

Use melted dark chocolate for dipping and drizzling:

1. Melt the dark chocolate in a microwave-safe bowl in 20-second intervals, stirring between each interval, until smooth and melted.
2. Dip one end of the cooled shortbread cookies into the melted chocolate and place them on parchment paper to set.
3. Use a fork or a piping bag to drizzle melted chocolate over the cooled cookies for an elegant touch.

Sea salt and dark chocolate shortbread is a testament to the elegant and refined flavors that can be achieved in a simple yet sophisticated cookie. By mastering the balance of buttery crumble, rich dark chocolate, and the touch of sea salt, you're creating cookies that offer a delightful sensory experience. In the next chapter, we'll explore the world of "No-Bake Cookies."

Chapter 11: Chocolate Oatmeal No-Bake Cookies

Prepare to embrace the joy of hassle-free cookie making with the beloved no-bake approach. In this chapter, we'll explore the art of crafting gluten-free no-bake cookies that deliver a decadent chocolate fix with the comforting addition of rolled oats.

Easy No-Bake Cookie Recipe

Ingredients:

- 1/2 cup unsalted butter
- 2 cups granulated sugar
- 1/2 cup milk or dairy-free alternative
- 1/4 cup unsweetened cocoa powder
- 1/2 cup creamy peanut butter
- 3 cups gluten-free rolled oats
- 1 teaspoon pure vanilla extract

Instructions:

1. Line a baking sheet with parchment paper.
2. In a large saucepan, combine the butter, sugar, milk, and cocoa powder. Bring to a boil over medium heat, stirring frequently.
3. Let the mixture boil for about 1-2 minutes, stirring constantly.
4. Remove the saucepan from heat and immediately stir in the peanut butter and vanilla extract until smooth.
5. Add the rolled oats and mix well until the oats are fully coated.
6. Drop spoonfuls of the mixture onto the prepared baking sheet.
7. Let the cookies cool and set at room temperature. They will firm up as they cool.

Incorporating Rolled Oats for Texture

Rolled Oats: The rolled oats provide a satisfying texture to these no-bake cookies. They add a chewy and hearty element that complements the rich chocolate.

Quick Oats: For a smoother texture, you can use quick oats instead of rolled oats. Keep in mind that the texture will be slightly different.

No-Bake Variations with Coconut, Nuts, and Fruits

Coconut Flakes: Add a tropical twist by folding in sweetened coconut flakes. They provide a pleasant chewiness and a hint of natural sweetness.

Chopped Nuts: Incorporate chopped nuts, such as walnuts or almonds, for added crunch and a nutty flavor.

Dried Fruits: Mix in dried fruits, like raisins, cranberries, or chopped apricots, to introduce a burst of fruity sweetness.

Quick and Decadent Chocolate Fix

These cookies are a perfect go-to for when you need a quick chocolate fix:

The no-bake approach means you can enjoy these cookies without waiting for them to bake.

They're an ideal treat to satisfy sudden chocolate cravings.

Chapter 12: Decadent Chocolate Avocado Cookies

Prepare to embark on a journey of guilt-free indulgence with the unique addition of avocado in these delicious chocolate cookies. In this chapter, we'll explore the art of crafting gluten-free cookies that achieve both creamy richness and a burst of healthiness.

Using Avocado for Creaminess and Healthiness

Ingredients:

- 1 ripe avocado, mashed
- 1/2 cup granulated sugar
- 1/4 cup unsweetened applesauce
- 1 large egg
- 1 teaspoon pure vanilla extract
- 1 1/2 cups gluten-free all-purpose flour
- 1/3 cup unsweetened cocoa powder
- 1/2 teaspoon baking soda
- 1/4 teaspoon salt
- 1/2 cup chocolate chips

Instructions:

1. Preheat your oven to 350°F (175°C) and line a baking sheet with parchment paper.
2. In a large bowl, whisk together the mashed avocado, granulated sugar, applesauce, egg, and vanilla extract until smooth.
3. In a separate bowl, whisk together the gluten-free flour, cocoa powder, baking soda, and salt.
4. Gradually add the dry ingredients to the wet ingredients, mixing until just combined.
5. Fold in the chocolate chips.

6. Drop spoonfuls of dough onto the prepared baking sheet, spacing them about 2 inches apart.
7. Bake for 10-12 minutes or until the edges are set. The centers may look slightly underdone, but they will firm up as they cool.
8. Allow the cookies to cool on the baking sheet for a few minutes before transferring them to a wire rack to cool completely.

Hiding Nutrients in Delicious Cookies

Avocado Goodness: Avocado brings a creamy and buttery texture to the cookies while providing a dose of healthy fats and nutrients.

Applesauce Magic: Unsweetened applesauce not only adds natural sweetness but also enhances the moistness of the cookies without the need for excess oil.

Balancing Chocolate and Avocado Flavors

Cocoa Harmony: The deep cocoa flavor of the cookies marries beautifully with the richness of avocado, creating a harmonious blend of indulgence and freshness.

Avocado Frosting and Fillings

Avocado Chocolate Frosting: Create a creamy frosting by blending mashed avocado, powdered sugar, and cocoa powder until smooth. Spread it over cooled cookies for an extra layer of richness.

Avocado Filling: Make avocado cream by blending mashed avocado, a touch of honey or maple syrup, and a pinch of salt. Use it as a filling for sandwich cookies.

Chapter 13: Gluten-Free Chocolate Sandwich Cookies

Get ready to explore the world of delightful sandwich cookies, where two gluten-free chocolate biscuits envelop a luscious filling. In this chapter, we'll dive into the art of crafting these delectable treats and explore various fillings and creative ways to present them.

Creating Cookie Sandwiches with Gluten-Free Biscuits
Ingredients for Biscuits:

- 1 1/2 cups gluten-free all-purpose flour
- 1/2 cup unsweetened cocoa powder
- 1/2 teaspoon baking powder
- 1/4 teaspoon salt
- 1/2 cup unsalted butter, softened
- 1 cup granulated sugar
- 1 large egg
- 1 teaspoon pure vanilla extract

Instructions for Biscuits:

1. Preheat your oven to 350°F (175°C) and line a baking sheet with parchment paper.
2. In a medium bowl, whisk together the gluten-free flour, cocoa powder, baking powder, and salt.
3. In a separate larger bowl, cream together the softened butter and granulated sugar until light and fluffy.
4. Beat in the egg and vanilla extract until well combined.
5. Gradually add the dry ingredients to the wet ingredients, mixing until just combined.
6. Roll out the dough on a lightly floured surface to about 1/4-inch thickness.

7. Use cookie cutters to cut out even-sized shapes for the top and bottom biscuits.
8. Place the biscuits on the prepared baking sheet and bake for 10-12 minutes or until the edges are set. The centers may look slightly underdone, but they will firm up as they cool.
9. Allow the biscuits to cool on the baking sheet for a few minutes before transferring them to a wire rack to cool completely.

Different Types of Fillings: Cream, Ganache, etc.

Cream Filling: Prepare a smooth and creamy filling using a combination of butter, powdered sugar, and a touch of vanilla extract.

Chocolate Ganache: Create a luxurious filling by melting together dark chocolate and heavy cream until smooth and glossy.

Nut Butter Spread: Spread almond butter, peanut butter, or cashew butter between the biscuits for a nutty and creamy twist.

Assembling and Decorating Cookie Sandwiches

Assembling: Once the biscuits have cooled, spread a generous amount of the chosen filling on the flat side of one biscuit. Place another biscuit on top, gently pressing to create a sandwich.

Decorating: Roll the edges of the sandwich cookies in colorful sprinkles, chopped nuts, or mini chocolate chips for an eye-catching and delicious touch.

Mini Cookie Sandwiches for Parties

For parties or gatherings, create mini versions of these delightful treats:

Use smaller cookie cutters to make bite-sized biscuits.

Create an assortment of fillings and allow guests to customize their own mini sandwich cookies.

Chapter 14: Chocolate Espresso Bites

Prepare to awaken your taste buds with the delightful marriage of chocolate and espresso. In this chapter, we'll explore the art of crafting gluten-free cookies that infuse the rich and aromatic flavor of coffee into every bite.

Adding Coffee Flavor for Depth
Ingredients:

- 1 1/2 cups gluten-free all-purpose flour
- 1/2 cup unsweetened cocoa powder
- 1/2 teaspoon baking powder
- 1/4 teaspoon salt
- 1 tablespoon espresso powder
- 1/2 cup unsalted butter, softened
- 1 cup granulated sugar
- 1 large egg
- 1 teaspoon pure vanilla extract

Instructions:

1. Preheat your oven to 350°F (175°C) and line a baking sheet with parchment paper.
2. In a medium bowl, whisk together the gluten-free flour, cocoa powder, baking powder, salt, and espresso powder.
3. In a separate larger bowl, cream together the softened butter and granulated sugar until light and fluffy.
4. Beat in the egg and vanilla extract until well combined.
5. Gradually add the dry ingredients to the wet ingredients, mixing until just combined.
6. Drop spoonfuls of dough onto the prepared baking sheet, spacing them about 2 inches apart.

7. Use a fork to gently press down on the dough to create a crisscross pattern.
8. Bake for 10-12 minutes or until the edges are set. The centers may look slightly underdone, but they will firm up as they cool.
9. Allow the cookies to cool on the baking sheet for a few minutes before transferring them to a wire rack to cool completely.

Incorporating Espresso Powder into Dough

Espresso Powder: This finely ground coffee powder adds a concentrated coffee flavor to the cookies. It's a key ingredient in achieving the desired espresso taste.

Adjusting Intensity: You can adjust the amount of espresso powder to control the strength of the coffee flavor.

Creating Chocolate Coffee Glazes

Chocolate Espresso Glaze: Create a glossy glaze by mixing together powdered sugar, cocoa powder, a touch of brewed espresso, and a dash of vanilla extract. Drizzle the glaze over the cooled cookies for an irresistible finish.

Mocha Glaze: Combine melted chocolate with brewed espresso for a decadent mocha glaze. Dip the cookies into the glaze for an even coating.

Espresso-Chocolate Energy Bites

Transform your chocolate espresso bites into energy-boosting snacks:

Ingredients:

- 1 cup gluten-free oats
- 1/2 cup almond butter
- 1/4 cup honey or maple syrup
- 2 tablespoons cocoa powder
- 1 tablespoon espresso powder
- 1/4 cup mini chocolate chips

Instructions:

1. In a mixing bowl, combine oats, almond butter, honey or maple syrup, cocoa powder, and espresso powder.
2. Fold in mini chocolate chips.
3. Roll the mixture into bite-sized balls and place them on a parchment-lined tray.
4. Refrigerate until firm, then enjoy as a quick and energizing treat.

Chapter 15: Hazelnut Chocolate Thumbprint Cookies

Get ready to create an irresistible fusion of nutty hazelnut flavors and luscious chocolate fillings in these charming thumbprint cookies. In this chapter, we'll delve into the art of crafting gluten-free cookies that are as visually appealing as they are delicious.

Crafting Thumbprint Indents for Fillings
Ingredients:

- 1 1/2 cups gluten-free all-purpose flour
- 1/2 cup hazelnut flour (or finely ground hazelnuts)
- 1/2 teaspoon baking powder
- 1/4 teaspoon salt
- 1/2 cup unsalted butter, softened
- 1/2 cup granulated sugar
- 1 large egg
- 1 teaspoon pure vanilla extract
- Chocolate fillings of your choice (e.g., Nutella, chocolate ganache)

Instructions:

1. Preheat your oven to 350°F (175°C) and line a baking sheet with parchment paper.
2. In a medium bowl, whisk together the gluten-free flour, hazelnut flour, baking powder, and salt.
3. In a separate larger bowl, cream together the softened butter and granulated sugar until light and fluffy.
4. Beat in the egg and vanilla extract until well combined.
5. Gradually add the dry ingredients to the wet ingredients, mixing until just combined.

6. Roll the dough into small balls and place them on the prepared baking sheet.
7. Use your thumb or the back of a teaspoon to gently press an indent in the center of each cookie.
8. Bake for 10-12 minutes or until the edges are set. The centers may look slightly underdone, but they will firm up as they cool.
9. Allow the cookies to cool on the baking sheet for a few minutes before transferring them to a wire rack to cool completely.

Nutella and Hazelnut Fillings

Nutella Filling: Fill the thumbprint indents with a dollop of Nutella for a creamy and indulgent center.

Chocolate Ganache: Create a rich chocolate ganache by melting together dark chocolate and heavy cream. Fill the indents with the ganache for a luxurious touch.

Hazelnut Spread: Combine finely ground toasted hazelnuts with a touch of honey to create a homemade hazelnut spread. Fill the cookies for a nutty and wholesome option.

Toasting Hazelnuts for Enhanced Flavor

Toasting Hazelnuts: Toast whole hazelnuts in the oven until they're fragrant and the skins start to crack. Rub the toasted hazelnuts in a kitchen towel to remove the skins, then finely grind them to make hazelnut flour.

Hazelnut Chocolate Thumbprint Cookie Variations

Fruit Filling: Experiment with fruit fillings like raspberry jam or apricot preserves for a delightful contrast to the nutty cookie.

Caramel Drizzle: After baking, drizzle caramel sauce over the cookies for an extra layer of decadence.

Chapter 16: Vegan Chocolate Coconut Cookies

Get ready to dive into the world of dairy-free delight with the heavenly combination of chocolate and coconut. In this chapter, we'll explore the art of crafting gluten-free vegan cookies that showcase the magic of coconut in all its forms.

Dairy-Free Chocolate and Coconut Creations
Ingredients:

- 1 1/2 cups gluten-free all-purpose flour
- 1/2 cup unsweetened cocoa powder
- 1/2 teaspoon baking powder
- 1/4 teaspoon salt
- 1/2 cup coconut oil, melted
- 1 cup granulated sugar (or coconut sugar for added coconut flavor)
- 1/4 cup coconut milk (canned, full fat)
- 1 teaspoon pure vanilla extract
- 1/2 cup shredded coconut (unsweetened)
- Dairy-free chocolate chips or chunks

Instructions:

1. Preheat your oven to 350°F (175°C) and line a baking sheet with parchment paper.
2. In a medium bowl, whisk together the gluten-free flour, cocoa powder, baking powder, and salt.
3. In a separate larger bowl, whisk together the melted coconut oil and granulated sugar until well combined.
4. Stir in the coconut milk and vanilla extract until smooth.
5. Gradually add the dry ingredients to the wet ingredients,

mixing until just combined.

6. Fold in the shredded coconut and dairy-free chocolate chips.
7. Drop spoonfuls of dough onto the prepared baking sheet, spacing them about 2 inches apart.
8. Flatten each cookie slightly with the back of a spoon.
9. Bake for 10-12 minutes or until the edges are set. The centers may look slightly underdone, but they will firm up as they cool.
10. Allow the cookies to cool on the baking sheet for a few minutes before transferring them to a wire rack to cool completely.

Coconut Milk and Oil in Vegan Baking

Coconut Milk: Canned, full-fat coconut milk adds creaminess to the cookies while infusing them with a subtle coconut flavor.

Coconut Oil: Use melted coconut oil as a dairy-free alternative to butter. It provides a rich and satisfying texture.

Vegan Chocolate Ganache and Icing

Vegan Chocolate Ganache: Create a dairy-free ganache by combining dairy-free chocolate and coconut cream. Use this ganache to fill the cookies or drizzle over the tops.

Coconut Icing: Make a simple coconut icing by whisking together powdered sugar and coconut milk until smooth. Drizzle the icing over the cooled cookies.

Coconut Whipped Cream for Toppings

Coconut Whipped Cream: Chill a can of full-fat coconut milk in the refrigerator. Open the can and scoop out the solid coconut cream at the top. Whip the coconut cream with a touch of powdered sugar and vanilla extract to create a luscious topping for your cookies.

Chapter 17: Chocolate Protein Power Cookies

Get ready to fuel your body and indulge your taste buds with the irresistible combination of chocolate and protein. In this chapter, we'll explore the art of crafting gluten-free cookies that are not only delicious but also packed with the power of protein.

Incorporating Protein-Rich Ingredients

Ingredients:

- 1 1/2 cups gluten-free all-purpose flour
- 1/2 cup chocolate protein powder
- 1/2 teaspoon baking powder
- 1/4 teaspoon salt
- 1/2 cup unsalted butter, softened
- 1/2 cup granulated sugar
- 1 large egg
- 1 teaspoon pure vanilla extract
- 1/2 cup chocolate chips or chunks

Instructions:

1. Preheat your oven to 350°F (175°C) and line a baking sheet with parchment paper.
2. In a medium bowl, whisk together the gluten-free flour, chocolate protein powder, baking powder, and salt.
3. In a separate larger bowl, cream together the softened butter and granulated sugar until light and fluffy.
4. Beat in the egg and vanilla extract until well combined.
5. Gradually add the dry ingredients to the wet ingredients, mixing until just combined.
6. Fold in the chocolate chips or chunks.

7. Drop spoonfuls of dough onto the prepared baking sheet, spacing them about 2 inches apart.
8. Flatten each cookie slightly with the back of a spoon.
9. Bake for 10-12 minutes or until the edges are set. The centers may look slightly underdone, but they will firm up as they cool.
10. Allow the cookies to cool on the baking sheet for a few minutes before transferring them to a wire rack to cool completely.

Balancing Taste and Nutrition

Flavor Harmony: While incorporating protein is essential, ensure that the cookies are still delicious and enjoyable to eat.

Sweeteners: Consider using natural sweeteners like honey or maple syrup to enhance sweetness while offering nutritional benefits.

Protein Powder in Gluten-Free Baking

Protein Powder Variety: opt for a high-quality chocolate protein powder that is gluten-free and suits your taste preferences.

Texture Consideration: Protein powder can affect the texture of the cookies. Balancing it with other ingredients is key to achieving the desired cookie texture.

Post-Workout Chocolate Protein Cookies

Make these cookies a part of your post-workout routine:

Refueling: After a workout, your body craves protein to aid muscle recovery. These cookies offer a delicious way to refuel.

Convenience: Bake a batch in advance and have them ready to enjoy after your workout session.

Chapter 18: Flourless Chocolate Almond Cookies

Get ready to savor the rich and nutty combination of chocolate and almonds in these delectable flourless cookies. In this chapter, we'll explore the art of crafting gluten-free cookies that rely on the goodness of almond flour and nut butters.

Almond Flour as a Gluten-Free Base

Ingredients:

- 2 cups almond flour
- 1/2 cup unsweetened cocoa powder
- 1 teaspoon baking soda
- 1/4 teaspoon salt
- 1/2 cup almond butter (or any nut butter)
- 1/2 cup honey or maple syrup
- 1 large egg
- 1 teaspoon pure almond extract
- 1/2 cup chocolate chips or chopped chocolate

Instructions:

1. Preheat your oven to 350°F (175°C) and line a baking sheet with parchment paper.
2. In a large bowl, whisk together the almond flour, cocoa powder, baking soda, and salt.
3. In a separate bowl, whisk together the almond butter, honey or maple syrup, egg, and almond extract until smooth.
4. Gradually add the wet ingredients to the dry ingredients, mixing until a dough forms.
5. Fold in the chocolate chips or chopped chocolate.
6. Drop spoonfuls of dough onto the prepared baking sheet,

spacing them about 2 inches apart.

7. Flatten each cookie slightly with the back of a spoon.
8. Bake for 10-12 minutes or until the edges are set. The centers may look slightly underdone, but they will firm up as they cool.
9. Allow the cookies to cool on the baking sheet for a few minutes before transferring them to a wire rack to cool completely.

Nut Butters for Flavor and Texture

Almond Butter: Almond butter enhances the nutty flavor of the cookies while contributing to their moist and chewy texture.

Variations: You can use other nut butters like peanut butter or cashew butter for different flavor profiles.

Almond Extract and Enhancing Almond Flavor

Almond Extract: A small amount of almond extract intensifies the almond flavor in the cookies, creating a more pronounced nutty taste.

Using Almond Flour: Almond flour not only adds nuttiness but also contributes to the soft and chewy texture of the cookies.

Flourless Almond Joy-Inspired Cookies

Coconut and Chocolate: Fold in shredded coconut along with the chocolate chips to capture the essence of an Almond Joy candy bar.

Nut Topping: Press a whole almond onto the top of each cookie before baking for a visual touch and an extra nutty crunch.

Chapter 19: Mexican Hot Chocolate Snickerdoodles

Prepare to embark on a journey of flavor and spice with the captivating fusion of Mexican hot chocolate and classic snickerdoodles. In this chapter, we'll explore the art of crafting gluten-free cookies that deliver a warm and spicy twist to a beloved favorite.

Spices for a Warm and Spicy Twist
Ingredients:

- 1 1/2 cups gluten-free all-purpose flour
- 1/2 cup unsweetened cocoa powder
- 1/2 teaspoon baking powder
- 1/4 teaspoon salt
- 1/2 teaspoon ground cinnamon
- 1/4 teaspoon ground cayenne pepper (adjust to taste)
- 1/2 cup unsalted butter, softened
- 1 cup granulated sugar
- 1 large egg
- 1 teaspoon pure vanilla extract

Instructions:

1. Preheat your oven to 350°F (175°C) and line a baking sheet with parchment paper.
2. In a medium bowl, whisk together the gluten-free flour, cocoa powder, baking powder, salt, ground cinnamon, and cayenne pepper.
3. In a separate larger bowl, cream together the softened butter and granulated sugar until light and fluffy.
4. Beat in the egg and vanilla extract until well combined.
5. Gradually add the dry ingredients to the wet ingredients,

mixing until just combined.

6. Drop spoonfuls of dough onto the prepared baking sheet, spacing them about 2 inches apart.

7. Roll each ball of dough in a mixture of granulated sugar and ground cinnamon to create the snickerdoodle coating.

8. Flatten each cookie slightly with the back of a spoon.

9. Bake for 10-12 minutes or until the edges are set. The centers may look slightly underdone, but they will firm up as they cool.

10. Allow the cookies to cool on the baking sheet for a few minutes before transferring them to a wire rack to cool completely.

Creating the Perfect Snickerdoodle Coating

Cinnamon Sugar Coating: The classic snickerdoodle coating consists of a mixture of granulated sugar and ground cinnamon. This coating creates the signature snickerdoodle flavor and appearance.

Adjusting Spice: The amount of cayenne pepper can be adjusted to suit your taste preference for spiciness. Start with a small amount and add more if desired.

Chocolate and Cinnamon Flavor Harmony

Mexican Hot Chocolate Inspiration: The combination of chocolate and cinnamon in these cookies draws inspiration from the flavors of Mexican hot chocolate, where the warmth of cinnamon complements the richness of chocolate.

Flavor Enhancements: The touch of cayenne pepper adds a subtle heat that elevates the flavor profile of these cookies.

Spicy Chocolate Cookie Pairings

Chai-Spiced Hot Chocolate: Pair these cookies with a cup of chai-spiced hot chocolate for a cozy and flavorful combination.

Vanilla Ice Cream: Serve the cookies alongside a scoop of dairy-free vanilla ice cream for a sweet and spicy dessert.

Chapter 20: Celebratory Chocolate Sprinkle Cookies

Prepare to bring joy and festivity to your taste buds with the delightful combination of chocolate and colorful sprinkles. In this final chapter, we'll explore the art of crafting gluten-free cookies that are perfect for celebrations and special occasions.

Festive and Colorful Sprinkle Decorations

Ingredients:

- 1 1/2 cups gluten-free all-purpose flour
- 1/2 cup unsweetened cocoa powder
- 1/2 teaspoon baking powder
- 1/4 teaspoon salt
- 1/2 cup unsalted butter, softened
- 1 cup granulated sugar
- 1 large egg
- 1 teaspoon pure vanilla extract
- Assorted colorful sprinkles

Instructions:

1. Preheat your oven to 350°F (175°C) and line a baking sheet with parchment paper.
2. In a medium bowl, whisk together the gluten-free flour, cocoa powder, baking powder, and salt.
3. In a separate larger bowl, cream together the softened butter and granulated sugar until light and fluffy.
4. Beat in the egg and vanilla extract until well combined.
5. Gradually add the dry ingredients to the wet ingredients, mixing until just combined.
6. Roll spoonfuls of dough into balls and roll each ball in a bowl

of colorful sprinkles to coat.

7. Place the sprinkle-coated dough balls on the prepared baking sheet, spacing them about 2 inches apart.
8. Flatten each cookie slightly with the back of a spoon.
9. Bake for 10-12 minutes or until the edges are set. The centers may look slightly underdone, but they will firm up as they cool.
10. Allow the cookies to cool on the baking sheet for a few minutes before transferring them to a wire rack to cool completely.

Incorporating Sprinkles into the Dough

Sprinkle Integration: For a hidden burst of color and fun, fold a small handful of sprinkles into the cookie dough before shaping it into balls.

Variations: Experiment with different types of sprinkles, from traditional rainbow sprinkles to themed shapes and colors.

Personalized Sprinkle Blends

DIY Sprinkles: Create your own custom sprinkle blends by mixing different colors, shapes, and sizes to match the theme of your celebration.

Special Occasions: Tailor your sprinkle blends to match holidays, birthdays, or other special events.

Sprinkle-Filled Piñata Cookies for Parties

Piñata Cookies: Create surprise-filled cookies by rolling out two dough circles for each cookie. On one circle, cut out a small shape (e.g., star, heart). Place the sprinkle-coated dough circle on top and press down to seal. When baked and broken, the colorful sprinkles will spill out like a piñata!

Party Favors: Bake a batch of piñata cookies and wrap them in individual bags as unique and delightful party favors.

And there you have it, a complete cookbook filled with an array of delicious gluten-free chocolate cookie recipes! From classic favorites to creative twists, each chapter explores a unique combination of flavors, techniques, and ingredients to create cookies that cater to various tastes and dietary preferences.

Throughout this cookbook, we've explored the magic of chocolate in its many forms, from rich cocoa powder to luscious, melted chocolate, combined with a variety of gluten-free flours and innovative ingredients. We've ventured into the realms of nutty textures, warm spices, and even the wonders of vegan and protein-packed options. These cookies aren't just treats; they're a celebration of the diverse world of chocolate and the joy it brings to our lives.

Whether you're baking for a special occasion, satisfying a chocolate craving, or simply seeking a delightful treat, you now have a comprehensive guide at your fingertips. From the moment you mix the ingredients to the final bite of each cookie, this cookbook is designed to spark creativity, inspire exploration, and fill your kitchen with the aroma of freshly baked delights.

Remember, the joy of baking lies not only in the final product but also in the journey itself. Feel free to experiment, personalize, and make each recipe your own. Share these cookies with loved ones, gather around a table, and savor the moments created by the act of baking and sharing.

Thank you for embarking on this culinary adventure with me. I hope this cookbook brings smiles, satisfaction, and a touch of sweetness to your life. Happy baking, and may your kitchen always be filled with the warmth and aroma of homemade gluten-free chocolate cookies!